BOOK 1

MW01098302

the POINTER SYSTEM

for the
Piano

A Fast, Easy and Direct Approach to the Learning of Chords and Melodies on the Piano

HAL•LEONARD®
CORPORATION
7777 W. BLUEMOUND RD. P.O. BOX 13819 MILWAUKEE, WI 53213

TABLE OF CONTENTS

SONGS

INTRODUCTION

This book is the beginning of a fascinating and rewarding adventure for you.

It is your introduction **To The POINTER SYSTEM**---the exciting and astonishingly easy method of learning to play the piano.

The POINTER SYSTEM teaches you to play the piano in a way that's **fun.** In an incredibly short time you will be playing songs you love, smoothly, skillfully, and with almost a professional touch. That will happen before you complete this book.

With **The POINTER SYSTEM** you play familiar melodies with full chord accompaniment right from the start, and you learn **AS YOU PLAY.** Your skill and your enjoyment will increase with every hour you spend at your piano.

The most wonderful aspect of your study in **The POINTER SYSTEM** is that it is a complete and thorough course in learning to play the piano---augmented by books of supplementary songs. So you have access to a great variety of music, all of which you can play using the keyboard knowledge you acquire in this and in the following Instruction Books of **The POINTER SYSTEM.**

With **The POINTER SYSTEM** you can learn to play the piano as you've always wished you could----even if you have never touched a keyboard before in your life. That's a promise that will begin to come true for you on the very next page of this book.

To Begin—

THIS IS THE KEYBOARD OF THE PIANO

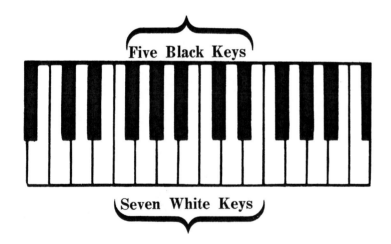

As the diagram to the left illustrates, the piano keyboard is a pattern of **seven white keys** and **five black keys** repeated over and over.

Also note that the white keys are evenly spaced and are interspersed with the black keys in a regular pattern; first a group of three, then a group of two; then three, then two, etc.

To make it even easier, each of the seven different white keys has a definite name. For these names we use the first seven letters of the alphabet repeated over and over. See the diagram to the right.

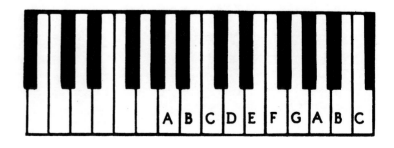

Further examination will show that you can use the black keys as reference points. You can find any particular white key by noting in which group of black keys it is found. Study the sections of keyboard below which point out the location of the first five notes you will be playing.

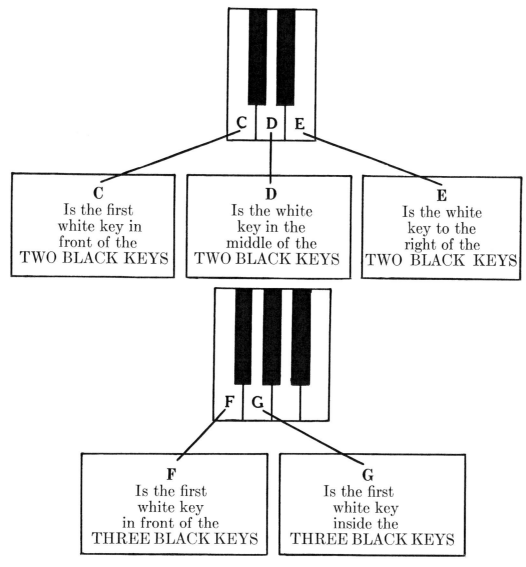

C
Is the first white key in front of the TWO BLACK KEYS

D
Is the white key in the middle of the TWO BLACK KEYS

E
Is the white key to the right of the TWO BLACK KEYS

F
Is the first white key in front of the THREE BLACK KEYS

G
Is the first white key inside the THREE BLACK KEYS

 Below is a section of the piano keyboard on which all the keys you will play in this book are marked. If you are unfamiliar with the keyboard, write the letter name on each key as shown on this diagram. Use a soft colored crayon or Listo pencil.

Notice the key marked **Middle C.** It is approximately in the center of the keyboard and even with the trademark. **Middle C** is commonly used as a reference point.

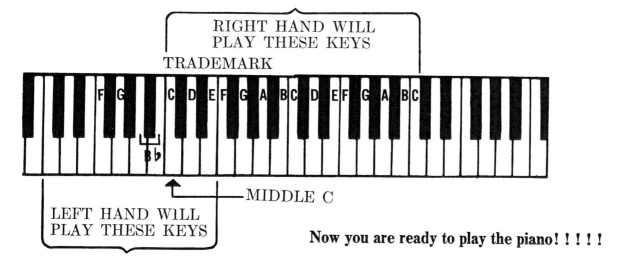

Now you are ready to play the piano ! ! ! !

The right hand plays these keys. Notice that the letter names of the notes match the letters on the keys.

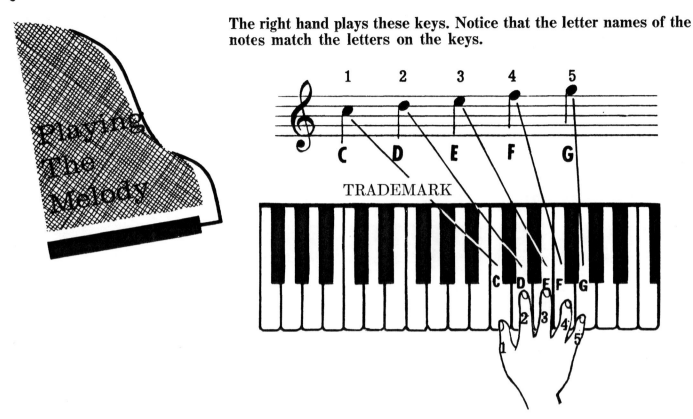

Now, let's play the melody of "Long, Long Ago" with the **right hand.** Starting with the thumb (No. 1), place your fingers on the keyboard exactly as in the diagram above. **Keep your hand in this position as you play! ! ! ! !**

Match the letter names of the notes with the letters on the keys. Strike a key for each note. The correct fingering is marked above each note.

LONG, LONG AGO

T. H. Bayly

The Pointer System

Now, let's find out what notes we play with the left hand. On the lower section of the keyboard, the left hand plays three notes together. We call this a "chord". We are going to learn to play chords by pointing to them. Playing a **Pointer Chord** is just as easy as pointing to an object in the room. Follow the directions below:

1st – With your "pointer finger" point to Middle C and press it down.

2nd – Move your thumb up two white keys to the right and press this note down.

3rd – Move your little finger down (to the left) three white keys and press this note down.

THIS IS THE Ⓒ CHORD ➡

Hold these three notes down.

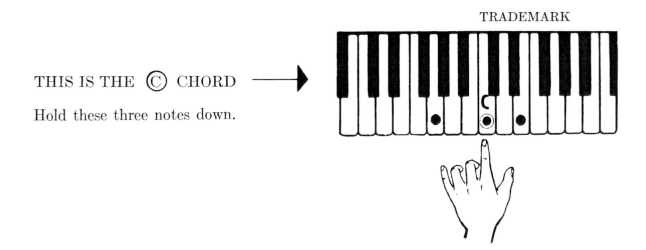

Now let's play the Ⓖ Chord------Play it exactly as you did the Ⓒ Chord except that this time point to Ⓖ ------The thumb two keys up to the right and the little finger three keys down to the left.

THIS IS THE Ⓖ CHORD ➡

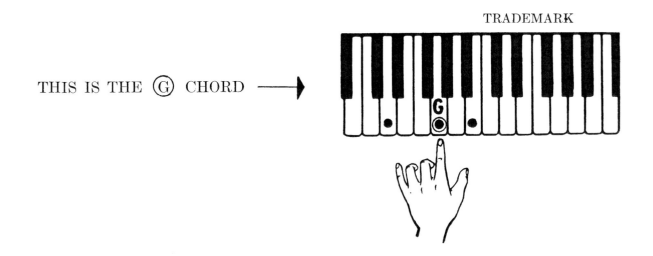

8

Now, you know a **melody** and two **chords.** Let's put them together. Keep these facts in mind:

● **Proper right hand fingering is indicated with small numbers above the melody notes.** Always use the correct fingering.

● **The correct chord is indicated above the melody in a circle.** When you see Ⓒ play the C Chord. When you see Ⓖ , play the G Chord.

● **A mark like this** ↓ **indicates that the chord you have been playing is to be played again.**

CHORDS USED IN THIS SONG:

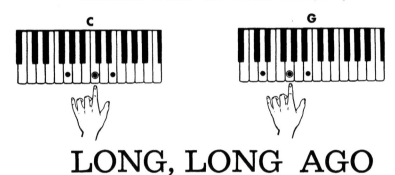

LONG, LONG AGO

T. H. Bayly

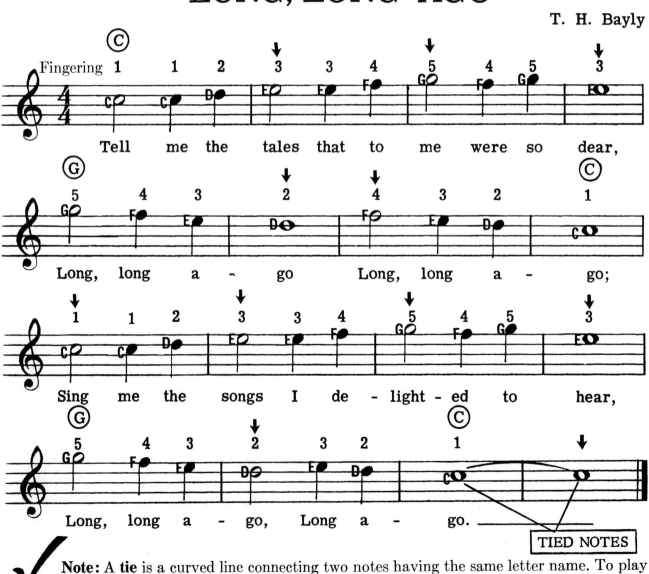

Note: A **tie** is a curved line connecting two notes having the same letter name. To play tied notes push the key down only once. Do not lift your finger to replay the note.

* ✔ **Here are a few facts about how music is written:**

Music is written on a series of lines and spaces called the **"staff"**. Lines above and below the staff are called **"ledger lines"**. The **"treble clef sign"** is placed at the beginning of each staff.

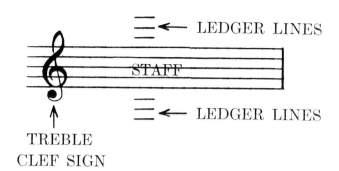

The music staff is divided into sections. Each section is called a **"measure"** and the dividing line is called a **"bar line"**.

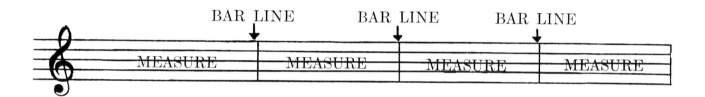

CHORDS USED IN THIS SONG:

MERRILY WE ROLL ALONG

* Watch for this sign (✔) for important facts worthy of your special attention and study.

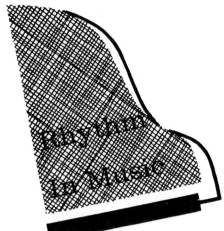

Music is composed of three parts-----melody, harmony and rhythm. The melody is the "tune" and the harmony is the "chord" that goes with the melody. Now, let's find out about the rhythm or "beat" in music.

We establish a definite rhythm in a song by counting a certain number of beats for each note. How many counts a note is given will depend on what the note looks like. Each kind of note has a name.

HERE ARE FOUR KINDS OF NOTES AND THEIR TIME VALUES.

♩	♩	♩.	𝅝
QUARTER NOTE 1 COUNT	HALF NOTE 2 COUNTS	DOTTED HALF NOTE 3 COUNTS	WHOLE NOTE 4 COUNTS

"Long, Long Ago" and "Merrily We Roll Along" sounded right to you because the tunes are familiar. Now, by learning how many counts or beats each kind of note gets, you will be able to play the rhythm correctly in any song.

Now, you are ready to play "Pop Goes The Weasel". The counting is indicated for you. There are three beats in every measure in this song.

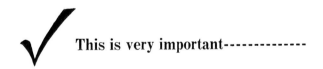 This is very important--------------

Count the beats aloud by saying 1-2-3-1-2-3-1-2-3 over and over. Always count evenly and rhythmically like the ticking of a clock.

Establish a good playing habit right now! ! ! ! !

ALWAYS

COUNT

ALOUD!!!!

When you start a new song, make it a habit to play each part separate-ly. Play the melody over several times first---then practice changing from one chord to another. **Good practice habits such as this will enable you to progress faster.**

CHORDS USED IN THIS SONG:

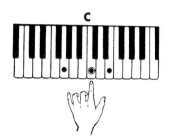   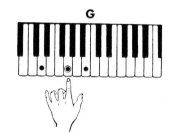

POP! GOES THE WEASEL

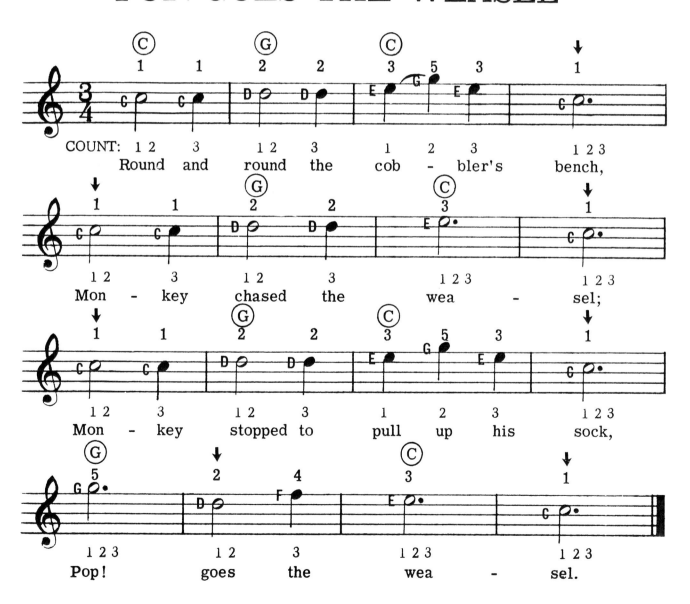

THE F CHORD

TRADEMARK

Here is a new chord------the F Chord. It's played the same as the "C" and "G" Chords, but this time point to "F".

CHORDS USED IN THIS SONG:

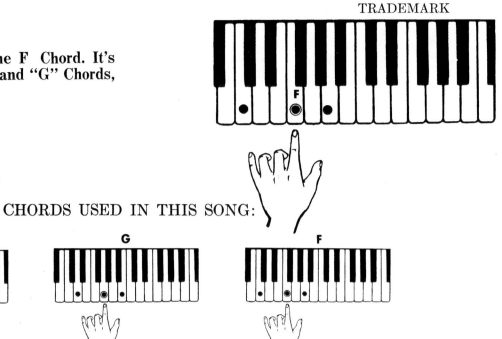

DRINK TO ME ONLY WITH THINE EYES

Traditional

---

* Beginning with this song you may use the sustaining pedal to achieve a fuller sounding tone. On Count 1 of each measure depress the sustaining pedal (the one farthest to the right) with your right foot.

The sustaining pedal will be studied in detail in Book 2.

Remember that the "POINTER" finger is the key to playing **THE POINTER SYSTEM WAY.** Always "point" to the chord.

The counting is indicated for you in the song below. There are **four** counts in each measure. Again count aloud. Also note that the fingering has been omitted where successive notes having the same letter name occur. You must lift your finger to repeat the note.

CHORDS USED IN THIS SONG:

JINGLE BELLS

Notes are placed either in a space or on a line.

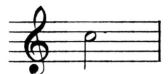

In a space----the note is placed **between** two lines.

On a line----the note is placed directly on the line.

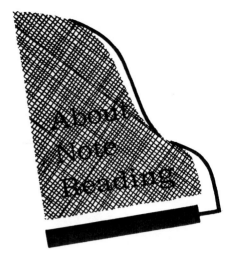

Each line or space on the staff gives the note a specific letter name. This letter name corresponds with the key having the same name. Look at the keyboard diagram below.

TRADEMARK

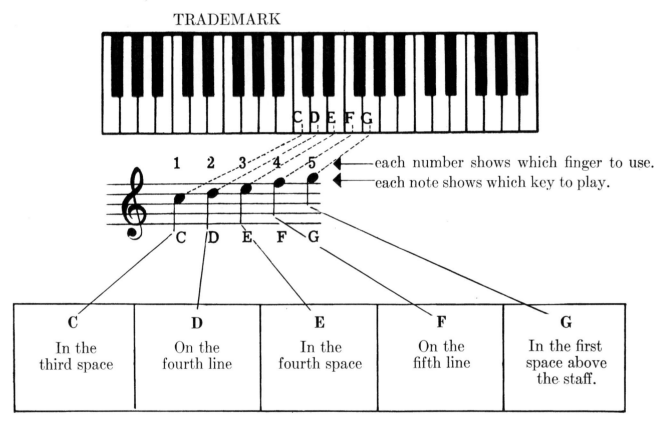

each number shows which finger to use.

each note shows which key to play.

C	D	E	F	G
In the third space	On the fourth line	In the fourth space	On the fifth line	In the first space above the staff.

 To progress faster and thus be able to play many more songs, it is important that you become a good note reader. A good note reader watches the distance between notes and always keeps his eyes on the music, looking at the keyboard only when necessary.

You have learned, from the keyboard diagram above, where five notes (CDEFG) are placed on the staff and where the five keys with those same names are located on the keyboard---so you already know something about note reading.

| DOWN means LOWER |

| UP means HIGHER |

When you move **down,** the notes go **down** on the staff; they sound **lower,** and your fingers move to the **left** or **down** the keyboard.

When you move **up,** the notes go **up** on the staff, they sound **higher** and your fingers move to the **right** or **up** the keyboard.

If a note moves from a space **up** to the next line, it is moving up one step------so play the next key with the next finger.

If a note moves from a space **up** to the next space, or from a line to the next line, it is skipping one note----so skip a key and skip a finger.

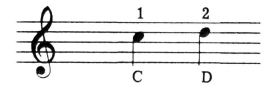

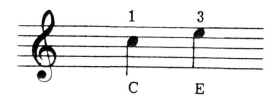

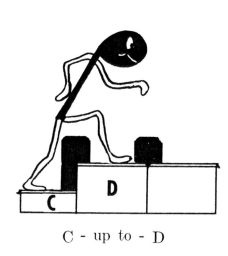

C - up to - D

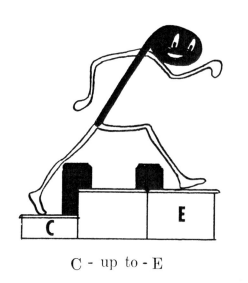

C - up to - E

Notes also move down on the staff.

When the notes move down, your fingers move down.

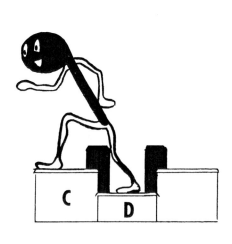

D - down to - C

E - down to - C

NOTE READING IS EASY.   JUST REMEMBER TO:

1. Keep the proper hand position on the five white keys as pictured on page 6.
2. Watch the distance from one note to the next.
3. Keep your eyes on the music.

Now------let's READ the notes as we play "Folk Song".

CHORDS USED IN THIS SONG:

FOLK SONG

The counting will not be indicated for you in the songs that follow-----but-----to give a good rhythmic "feel" to your playing-----**you keep counting ! ! !**

Here's how you will know how many counts there are in each measure. Look for the **two numbers** at the beginning of the first staff of each song. This is the **time signature.**

THE TOP NUMBER WILL TELL YOU HOW MANY COUNTS THERE ARE IN EACH MEASURE.

3/4-means **three** counts in each measure
-means the quarter note gets one count

4/4-means **four** counts in each measure
-means the quarter note gets one count

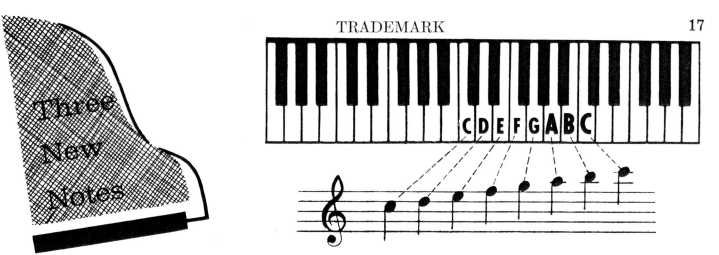

Now you have eight notes to play and you will have to start moving your hand to different positions on the keyboard. In all the other songs you played E with finger No. 3. Now, look at the song below. Isn't the first note E? But notice that the number above the note tells you to play it with finger No. 2.

Do just what the notes tell you-----Play E with finger No. 2, keep the rest of your fingers in place in this **new** position, watch how the notes move and this song will be just as easy as the others.

CHORDS USED IN THIS SONG:

DU, DU, LIEGST MIR IM HERZEN

Using all the notes we now know, let's play with the C Scale.
Watch the fingering carefully.

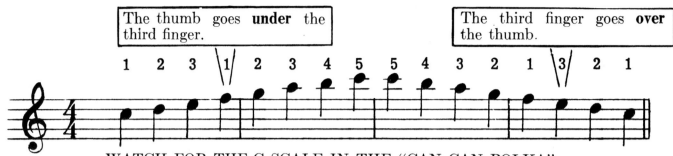

WATCH FOR THE C SCALE IN THE "CAN CAN POLKA".

In this song you will use all the notes you have learned thus far. Do you know the placement of each note on the staff, its letter name and corresponding key on the keyboard? Study three notes each day. You will soon be able to recognize them easily.

CHORDS USED IN THIS SONG:

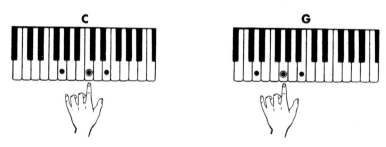

CAN CAN POLKA

Do you know the different kinds of notes? Correctly identify the notes below. The first one is done for you.

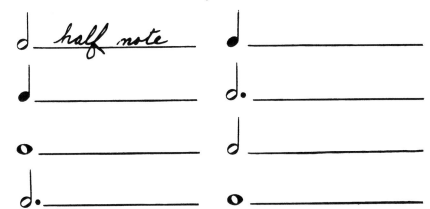

Fill in the missing words in the statements below:

1. The melody is played with the_____hand.
2. The chords are played with the_____hand.
3. A_____note gets two counts.
4. A_____note gets four counts.
5. A_____note gets one count.
6. A_____note gets three counts.
7. The distance between two bar lines is called a_____.
8. When two notes with the same name are joined together with a curved line, they are called_____notes.
9. The series of lines and spaces on which music is written is called the_____.
10. Lines above or below the staff are called_____lines.

(answers on page 23)

You have played eight different notes on the treble clef staf. Test your knowledge of the letter names of these notes by doing the exercises below. Remember that you must recognize a note by its position on the staff.

On the staff below cross out any note which is incorrectly labeled.

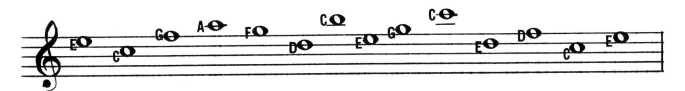

Write the correct letter names of the notes on the staff below.
The first one is done for you.

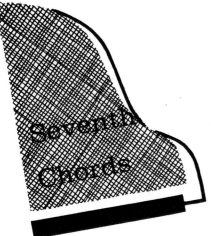

Now let's learn to play seventh chords. We will start with the G Seventh. The G Seventh is the same as the G Chord except that you add one more note.

Play the G Chord and then place the third (or middle) finger on the white key next to the "Pointer" finger. Press down the four keys. The seventh chord will be indicated by the number 7 after the letter name of the chord.

The G7 looks like this:

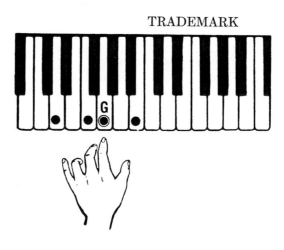

With the D Seventh Chord you use a black key for the first time. Follow the same procedure for finding this chord as you did for the other chords.

1. "Point" to D with the index or pointer finger.

2. Move the thumb up two white keys **but in the D7 Chord place it on the black key just above the second white key.**

3. Place the little finger three white keys below the pointer finger **and**

4. Place the middle finger (No 3) on the white key next to the pointer finger.

The D7 Chord looks like this:

NOTE: In order to keep a relaxed and comfortable hand position when playing on the black keys, place your finger well toward the back of the keyboard.

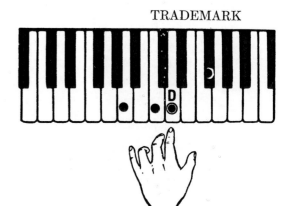

Play the G Seventh Chord (G7) in the song below:

CHORDS USED IN THIS SONG:

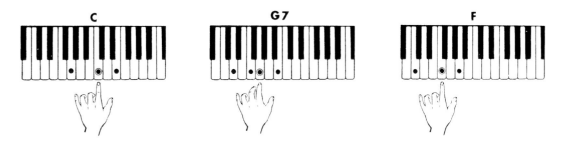

OH! SUSANNA

Stephen Foster

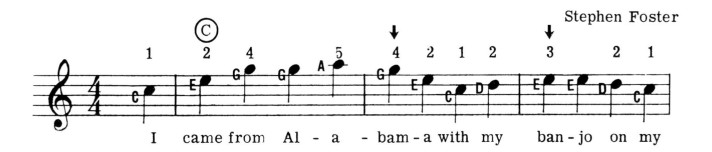

I came from Al - a - bam-a with my ban-jo on my

knee, I'm goin' to Lou'-si - a - na, My___ true love for to

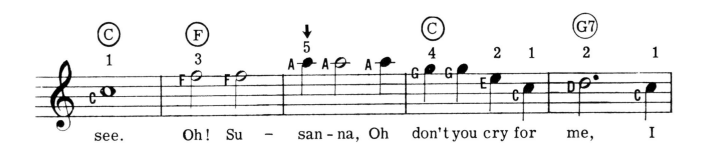

see. Oh! Su - san-na, Oh don't you cry for me, I

come from A - la - bam-a with my ban-jo on my knee.

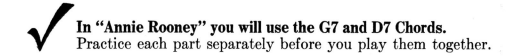

In "Annie Rooney" you will use the G7 and D7 Chords.
Practice each part separately before you play them together.

CHORDS USED IN THIS SONG:

ANNIE ROONEY

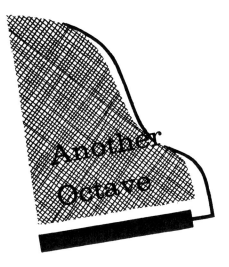

Thus far your playing has been confined to a range of eight notes--- from the C in the third space to the C on the second line above the staff.

These eight notes are called an **octave.** Now let's add another octave to your playing range.

Study carefully the new octave below. Again learn each note by its placement on the staff and its corresponding key on the keyboard.

TRADEMARK

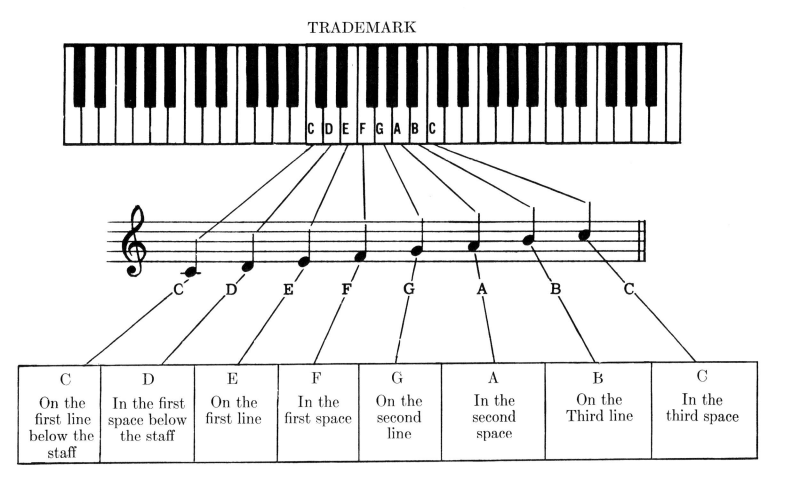

C	D	E	F	G	A	B	C
On the first line below the staff	In the first space below the staff	On the first line	In the first space	On the second line	In the second space	On the Third line	In the third space

answers for quiz on page 19

1. right
2. left
3. half
4. whole
5. quarter
6. dotted half
7. measure
8. tied
9. staff
10. ledger

✔ **This is a QUARTER REST:** 𝄽

The quarter rest gets one count just as the quarter note does.
When you see this sign, do not play but rest for one count.

FIND THE QUARTER RESTS IN THE LAST MEASURE OF "DOWN IN THE VALLEY".

CHORDS USED IN THIS SONG:

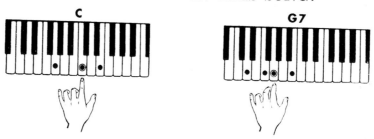

DOWN IN THE VALLEY

Traditional

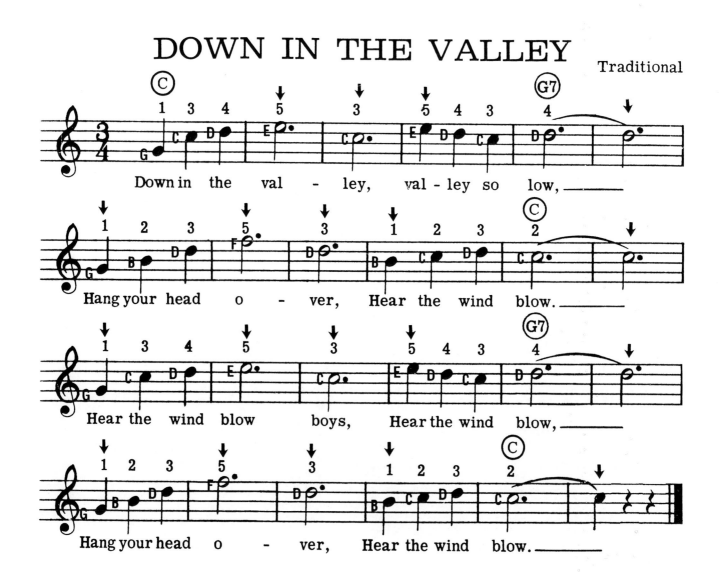

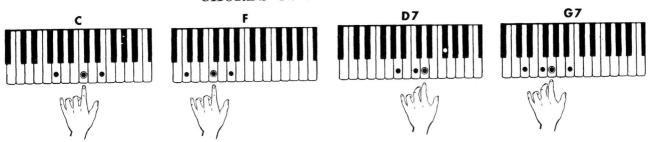

CHORDS USED IN THIS SONG:

FAITH OF OUR FATHERS

Hemy-Walton

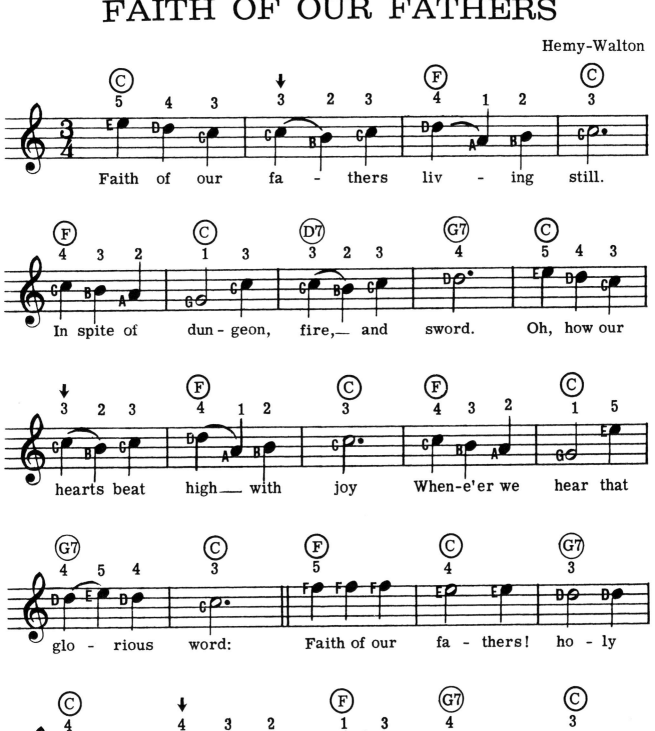

One eighth note is written like this:

Two or more eighth notes are usually written like this:

One quarter note	=	1 count
Two eighth notes	=	1 count
One eighth note	=	1/2 count

Thus two eighth notes are played in the same time as one quarter note.

Here is an explanation of how the quarter note (or 1 count) is divided when playing eighth notes.

The quarter note (or 1 count) consists of a **downbeat** and an **upbeat.** which can be diagramed like this:

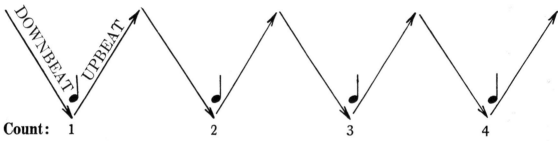

In playing eighth notes we divide the count into halves with one eighth note on the **downbeat** and another on the **upbeat.** To play them evenly and accurately we count:

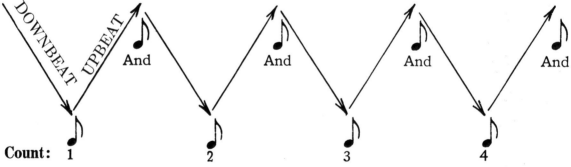

Play the right hand melody below:

27

Sometimes we have one or more notes at the beginning of a song which are not a complete measure. We call these **"pick up notes".** The number of counts which the pick up notes get are taken from the last measure of the song. Watch for pick up notes in some of the songs that follow.

ARE YOU COUNTING ALOUD AS YOU PLAY?

CHORDS USED IN THIS SONG:

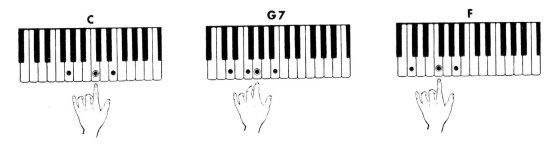

LITTLE BROWN CHURCH IN THE VALE

28

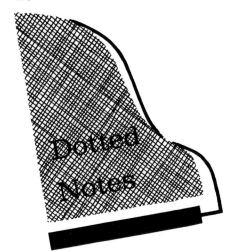

A dot after a note increases its value by one-half.

$\dotted{} = \half + \quarter = $ 3 counts $\quad \dotted{} = \quarter + \eighth = $ 1-1/2 counts

Note, in the example above, that the **quarter** and **eighth** tied together have the same time value as the **dotted quarter.**

Play the first two measures below--------Now play the last two measures.

The only difference between the first two measures and the last two measures is the way they are written. **They sound the same and are counted the same.**

Now play the song below using eighth notes and dotted quarter notes.
Play the melody several times alone and count aloud ! ! ! !

CHORDS USED IN THIS SONG:

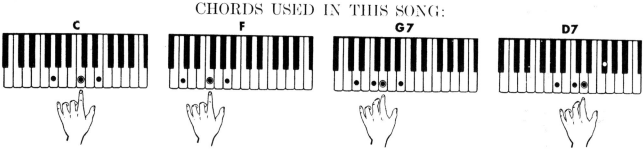

ANDANTINO

E. H. Lemare

ROSE OF TRALEE

C. W. Glover

All the songs you have played to this point have been written in the Key of C Major. This means that the melodies and chords in these songs are built around the C Major Scale.

Now you are going to play in the Key of F Major and the melodies and chords will be built around the F Major Scale.

The pattern of sound for the F Major Scale is the same as the C Major Scale, the only difference being that the F Scale sounds higher. (Review the C Scale on page 18).

In order to play the same pattern of sound it will be necessary to play a **black key.** This black key is Bb (B flat). As the diagram below indicates, Bb is the black key directly to the left of B on the keyboard.

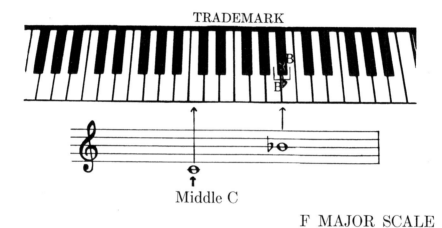

Middle C

F MAJOR SCALE

Now, to get the "feel" of the new key play the F Major Scale.

 Here are two new chords which you will play with songs written in the Key of F Major. Follow the same procedure for playing these chords as you did for the others.

1. "Point" to Bb with the **pointer** finger (Bb is the black key just to the left of B).
2. Move the thumb up three white keys to D.
3. Place the little finger three keys below the **pointer** finger on F.

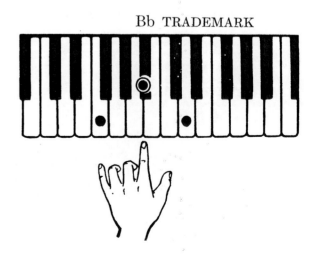

Bb TRADEMARK

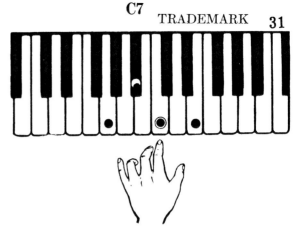

The C7 Chord is the same as the C Chord except that you add one more note. Play the C Chord and place the third or middle finger on the first black key below the **pointer** finger (Bb).

"Carnival of Venice" is written in the Key of F Major. The flat placed at the beginning of the staff on the third line (the B line) is called the **key signature.** It indicates that all B's are to be played as Bb (B flat).

CHORDS USED IN THIS SONG:

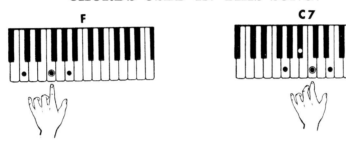

CARNIVAL OF VENICE

Play Bb in this song

* When melody and chord tones overlap, omit the chord tone and play the note with the right hand.

CHORDS USED IN THIS SONG:

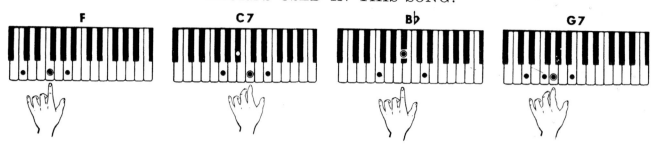

BEAUTIFUL DREAMER

Stephen Foster

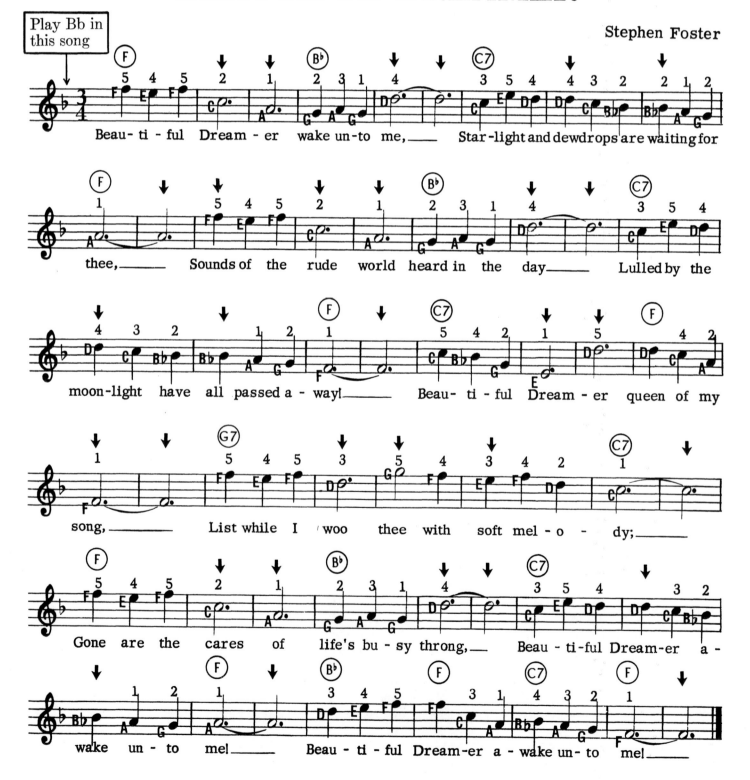

You have added many new "musical words" to your vocabulary. Let's review them by taking this matching test.

In the left column below are musical terms and definitions. Read each term or definition. Then select from the column on the right, the word (or symbol) which has the same meaning. Place the letter of the correct answer in the bracket. The first one is done for you.

1. (q) Treble clef   (a) **4/4**

2. ( ) Half note   (b) 𝄽

3. ( ) Tied notes   (c) ♩

4. ( ) The staff   (d) Fingering

5. ( ) Quarter note   (e) Seventh chord

6. ( ) Time signature   (f) Pick up notes

7. ( ) Quarter rest   (g) Measure

8. ( ) Dotted half note   (h) Ledger lines

9. ( ) A range of eight notes   (i) ♩.

10. ( ) Whole note   (j) ↓

11. ( ) Chord symbol   (k) ☰

12. ( ) Line added above or below staff   (l) 𝅗𝅥

13. ( ) Numbers above notes   (m) ♩.

14. ( ) A chord having four notes   (n) 𝅝

15. ( ) Eighth note   (o) Octave

16. ( ) Symbol meaning to replay a chord   (p) ©

17. ( ) The "beat" or pulse in music   (q) 𝄞

18. ( ) Dotted quarter note   (r) 𝅗𝅥. 𝅗𝅥.

19. ( ) The distance between two bar lines   (s) Rhythm

20. ( ) Note or notes before the first full measure of a song   (t) ♪

Answers on page 35

CHORDS USED IN THIS SONG:

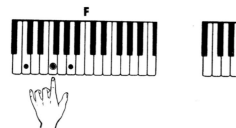
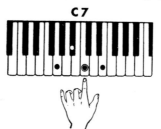
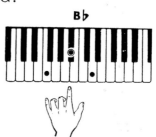

BELIEVE ME IF ALL THOSE
ENDEARING YOUNG CHARMS

Thomas Moore

Play Bb in this song.

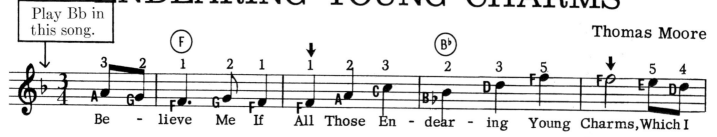

Be - lieve Me If All Those En - dear - ing Young Charms, Which I

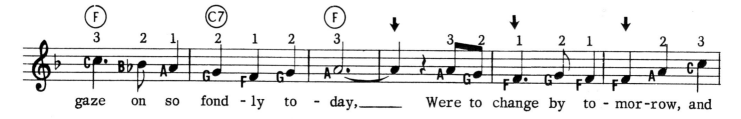

gaze on so fond - ly to - day,____ Were to change by to - mor - row, and

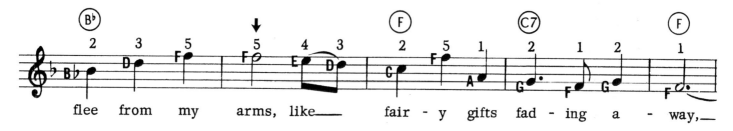

flee from my arms, like____ fair - y gifts fad - ing a - way,____

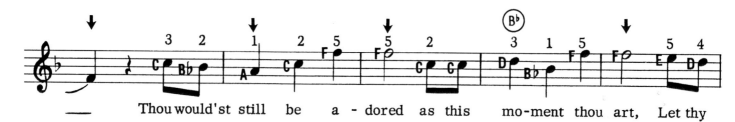

____ Thou would'st still be a - dored as this mo - ment thou art, Let thy

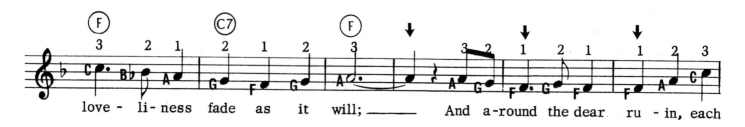

love - li - ness fade as it will;____ And a - round the dear ru - in, each

wish of my heart would en - twine it - self ver - dant - ly still._____

CHORDS USED IN THIS SONG:

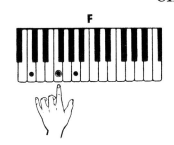
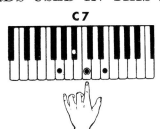
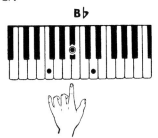

HOME SWEET HOME

H. R. Bishop

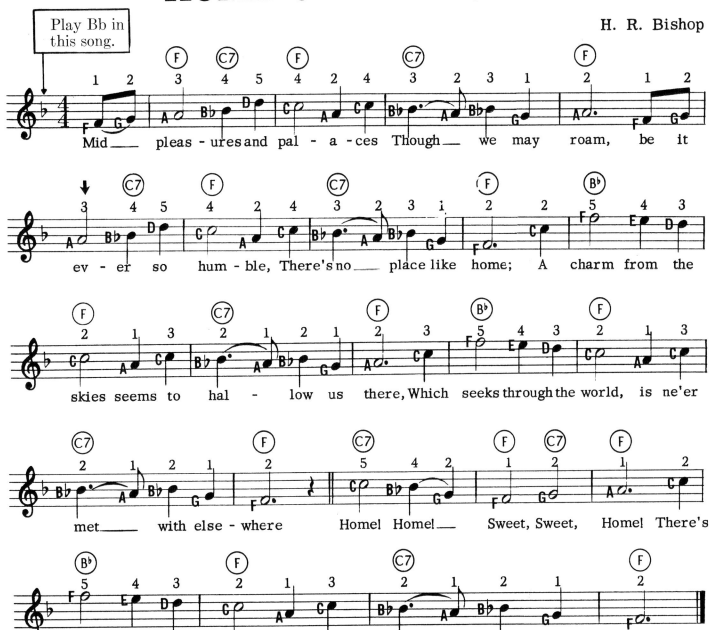

CHORDS USED IN THIS SONG:

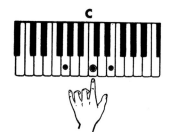
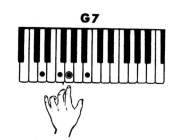
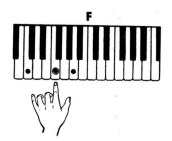

AULD LANG SYNE

Traditional

Should auld ac-quaintance be for-got, and nev-er brought to mind? Should auld ac-quain-tance

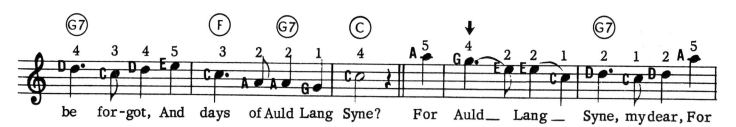

be for-got, And days of Auld Lang Syne? For Auld__ Lang__ Syne, my dear, For

Auld__ Lang__ Syne, We'll tak' a cup o' kind-ness yet For__ Auld__ Lang__ Syne.

You have now completed Book 1 of the POINTER SYSTEM for learning to play the piano. You are already playing many familiar songs with ease, even though you have learned only a few basic chords.

Book 2 of the **POINTER SYSTEM** will introduce many new chords which will add hundreds of songs to your repertoire. You will learn how to play rhythms as well as many other new techniques for the piano **and** you will soon be able to play with ease many of the currently popular and standard songs published.

The **POINTER SYSTEM** is your key to a personal enjoyment of music you never before thought possible. Its continued study will, in the shortest possible time, give you a playing ability you have always dreamed of.

FOR MORE INFORMATION, SEE YOUR LOCAL MUSIC DEALER, OR WRITE TO:

HAL•LEONARD®
CORPORATION
7777 W. BLUEMOUND RD. P.O. BOX 13819 MILWAUKEE, WI 53213